WiT

THE GREATEST THINGS EVER SAID

WiT

Leonard Roy Frank

RANDOM HOUSE
REFERENCE

INTRODUCTION

*I*f only there were a mathematics of wit, for example, two half-wits equal one wit, the subject of wit would be much easier to explain and understand. But wit stems from the imagination where there are few laws and formulas, and even those are flexible and apt to change without warning, often to the embarrassment of those who rely on them too much.

The imagination is like a cauldron where ideas and words are mixed together and processed into sentences. Almost all of these sentences are humdrum and calculated to serve some immediate, everyday need, but every once in a while there emerges from the cauldron a magical combination of words that makes us laugh or think. And there we have the stuff of wit, which may be defined as clever, sharp, insightful, or amusing observations or remarks intended to tickle the funny bone (ha-ha wit) or provoke thought (a-ha wit). Tallulah Bankhead's "If I had to live my life again, I'd make the same mistakes—only sooner" falls into the category of ha-ha wit. Winston Churchill's "Democracy is the worst form of government except all those other forms that have been tried from time to time" exemplifies a-ha wit.

Assembled in this book are nearly three hundred examples of wit from the works of well-known wit-meisters like Mark Twain, George Bernard Shaw, and Woody Allen, to those of lesser-known ones like Artemus Ward, Kin Hubbard, and Fran Lebowitz. There are also witticisms from figures well known in their own right but not necessarily as wits, such as George Washington, Ralph Waldo Emerson, and Mother Jones, and from entertainers, such as Lilly Tomlin, George Carlin, and David Letterman. Lastly, we can't forget that most prolific of contributors to the world's body of wit: Mr./Ms. Anonymous, who is well represented in this collection.

So have a good read, and if you derive half as much pleasure in perusing this book as I had in producing it, I'm sure you will feel it was worth the effort.

THERE IS NO CURE for birth and death save to enjoy the interval.

George Santayana, Spanish-born U.S. philosopher, 1863–1952

Life is what happens to you while you're busy making other plans.

John Lennon, English singer and songwriter, 1940–1980

If I had to live my life again, I'd make the same mistakes—*only sooner.*

Tallulah Bankhead, U.S. actor, 1903–1965

ABSTINENCE is a good thing, but it should always be practiced in moderation.

Anonymous

Instant gratification takes too long.

Carrie Fisher, contemporary U.S. actor and writer

$\mathcal{S}$CHOOL is about two parts ABCs to fifty parts Where Do I Stand in the Great Pecking Order of Humankind.

Barbara Kingsolver, contemporary U.S. writer

Colleges are like old-age homes, except for the fact that more people die in colleges.

Bob Dylan, contemporary U.S. songwriter and singer

I HAVE FOUND the best way to give advice to your children is to find out what they want, and then advise them to do it.

Harry S. Truman, U.S. president, 1884–1972

The most important thing in acting is honesty: if you can fake that, you've got it made.

George Burns, U.S. comedian, 1896–1996 (attributed)

Better to be pissed off than pissed on.

Michel Paul Richard, contemporary U.S. writer

5

REALITY is a crutch for people who can't deal with drugs.

Lily Tomlin, contemporary U.S. comedian and actor

Reality is that which, when you stop believing in it, *doesn't go away.*

Philip K. Dick, U.S. writer, 1928–1982

THERE ARE THREE KINDS OF PEOPLE: those who make things happen, those who wait for things to happen, and those who wonder what the hell happened.

Anonymous

THERE ARE ONLY TWO KINDS OF COMPUTER USERS: those who have lost data in a crash, and those who will lose data in a crash.

Bob LeVitus, contemporary U.S. writer

The real danger is not that computers will begin to think like men, but that men will begin to think like computers.

Sydney J. Harris, English-born U.S. journalist, 1917–1986

1. THE INFORMATION WE HAVE IS NOT WHAT WE WANT.
2. THE INFORMATION WE WANT IS NOT WHAT WE NEED.
3. THE INFORMATION WE NEED IS NOT AVAILABLE.

Finagle's New Laws of Information, 1979

There are two kinds of statistics: the kind you look up and the kind you make up.

Rex Stout, U.S. writer, 1886–1975

Death and taxes and childbirth! There's never any convenient time for any of them.

Margaret Mitchell, U.S. writer, 1900–1949

WHATEVER WOMEN DO, they must do twice as well as men to be thought half as good. Luckily, this is not difficult.

Charlotte Whitton, Ottawa mayor, 1896–1975

Walking on water wasn't built in a day.

Jack Kerouac, U.S. writer, 1922–1969

I love mankind—*it's people I can't stand.*

Charles M. Schulz, U.S. cartoonist, 1922–2000

THIS WORLD is a comedy to those that think, a tragedy to those that feel.

Horace Walpole, English writer, 1717–1797

Tragedy is if I cut my finger. Comedy is if you walk into an open sewer and die.

Mel Brooks, contemporary U.S. writer, actor, and film director

Comedy is tragedy that happens to other people.

Angela Carter, English journalist, 1940–1992

AN idea isn't responsible for the people who believe in it.

Don Marquis, U.S. journalist and humorist, 1878–1937

We are never so certain of our knowledge as when we're dead wrong.

Adair Lara, contemporary U.S. journalist

The trouble with the world is that the stupid are cocksure and the intelligent full of doubt.

Bertrand Russell, English mathematician and philosopher, 1872–1970

The tragedy of the world is that those who are imaginative have but slight experience, and those who are experienced have feeble imaginations.

Alfred North Whitehead, English mathematician and philosopher, 1861–1947

WE OWE A LOT to Thomas Edison. Were it not for him, we'd all be watching television by candlelight.

Milton Berle, U.S. comedian, 1908–2002 (attributed)

The minds that control television are so small that you could put them in the navel of a flea and still have room for a network vice president's heart.

Fred Allen, U.S. comedian, 1894–1956

I find television very educational. Every time someone switches it on, I go into another room and read a good book.

Groucho Marx, U.S. comedian, actor, and television personality, 1895–1977

14

THE wise talk because they have something to say: fools, because they have to say something.

Plato, Greek philosopher, fourth century B.C. (attributed)

It's better to keep your mouth shut and appear stupid than to open it and *remove all doubt.*

Mark Twain, U.S. writer and humorist, 1835–1910

YOU CAN FOOL some of the people all of the time and all of the people some of the time, but you can make a damn fool of yourself any old time.

Laurence J. Peter, Canadian academic and writer, 1919–1990

A man loses his illusions first, his teeth second, and his follies last.

Helen Rowland, U.S. journalist and humorist, 1875–1950

When a true genius appears in the world, you may know him by this sign, that the dunces are all in confederacy against him.

Jonathan Swift, English clergyman and writer, 1667–1745

SOMETIMES, especially if we are too lucky or too successful or too pretty, our misery is the only thing that endears us to our friends.

Erica Jong, contemporary U.S. writer

When you are down and out, something always turns up—and it's usually the noses of your friends.

Orson Welles, U.S. writer, actor, and film director, 1915–1985

THE trouble with most folks ain't so much their ignorance, as knowing so many things that ain't so.

Josh Billings, U.S. writer and humorist, 1818–1885

Education is learning what you didn't even know you didn't know.

Daniel J. Boorstin, contemporary U.S. historian

EDUCATION, N. That which discloses to the wise and disguises from the foolish their lack of understanding.

Ambrose Bierce, U.S. journalist and writer, 1842–1914

It's what we learn after we think we know it all that counts.

Kin Hubbard, U.S. journalist and humorist, 1868–1930

Nothing is ever so bad that it can't get worse.

Gattuso's Extension of Murphy's Law, 1980

Wherever and whenever one person is found adequate to the discharge of a duty by close application thereto, it is worse executed by two persons, and scarcely done at all if three or more are employed therein.

George Washington, U.S. president, 1732–1799 (letter, 1792)

We all know the rule of umbrellas—if you take your umbrella, it will not rain; if you leave it, it will.

Ralph Waldo Emerson, U.S. philosopher, 1803–1882

Problems worthy
of attack
prove their worth
by hitting back.

*Piet Hein, Danish scientist
and poet, 1905–1996*

REAL PROBLEMS HAVE NO SOLUTIONS.

Anonymous

Henry Clay is so brilliant yet so corrupt that, like a rotten mackerel by moonlight, *he both shines and stinks.*

John Randolph, Virginia congressman, 1773–1833

Clement Attlee reminds me of nothing so much as a recently dead fish, before it has had time to stiffen.

George Orwell, English writer, 1903–1950

CLEMENT ATTLEE IS a modest man who has a good deal to be modest about.

Winston Churchill, British prime minister, 1874–1965 (attributed)

Lenin is one of those politicians who win an undeserved reputation by dying prematurely.

George Orwell, English writer, 1903–1950

Following Eleanor Roosevelt in search of irrationality is like following a burning fuse in search of an explosive; *one never has to wait very long.*

William F. Buckley Jr., contemporary U.S. writer and publisher

WARREN HARDING WRITES THE WORST ENGLISH that I have ever encountered.

It reminds me of a string of wet sponges; it reminds me of tattered washing on the line; it reminds me of stale bean soup, of college yells, of dogs barking idiotically through endless nights. It is so bad that a sort of grandeur creeps into it. It drags itself out of the dark abysm of pish and crawls insanely up to the topmost pinnacle of posh. It is rumble and bumble. It is flap and doodle. It is balder and dash.

H. L. Mencken, U.S. journalist and critic, 1880–1956

RICHARD NIXON IS THE kind of politician who would cut down a redwood tree, then mount the stump for a speech on conservation.

Adlai E. Stevenson, Illinois governor, presidential candidate and UN ambassador, 1900–1965

The only gracious way to accept an insult is to ignore it; if you can't ignore it, top it; if you can't top it, laugh at it; if you can't laugh at it, it's probably deserved.

Russell Lynes, contemporary U.S. editor

*T*HE secret of rulership is to combine a belief in one's infallibility with the power to learn from past mistakes.

George Orwell, English writer, 1903–1950

Politics, *n.* A strife of interests masquerading as a contest of principles. The conduct of public affairs for private advantage.

Ambrose Bierce, U.S. journalist and writer, 1842–1914

He knows nothing, and he thinks he knows everything. That points clearly to a political career.

George Bernard Shaw, British playwright and critic, 1856–1950

A politician should have three hats: one for throwing in the ring, one for talking through, and one for pulling rabbits out of if elected.

Carl Sandburg, U.S. poet and writer, 1874–1965

I ASKED A MAN IN PRISON ONCE

how he happened to be there and he said he had stolen a pair of shoes. I told him if he had stolen a railroad he would be a United States senator.

Mother Jones (Mary Harris Jones), Irish-born U.S. labor leader, 1830–1930

Our senator was of that stuff that our best hope lay in his drunkenness, as that sometimes incapacitated him from doing mischief.

Ralph Waldo Emerson, U.S. philosopher, 1803–1882

BUT shucks, we got the best politicians in this country that money can buy.

Will Rogers, U.S. writer, actor, and humorist, 1879–1935

An honest politician is one who when he is bought will stay bought.

Simon Cameron, Pennsylvania senator and secretary of war, 1799–1889

REASONS WHY MEMBERS OF Congress

deserve a pay rise: many big corporations are cutting back on bribes; nearly half the members have never been indicted.

David Letterman, contemporary U.S. television talk-show host

IT COULD PROBABLY BE SHOWN BY FACTS AND FIGURES THAT THERE IS NO DISTINCTLY NATIVE AMERICAN CRIMINAL CLASS EXCEPT CONGRESS.

Mark Twain, U.S. writer and humorist, 1835–1910

THE difference between a politician and statesman is: A politician thinks of the next election and a statesman thinks of the next generation.

James Freeman Clarke, U.S. clergyman, 1810–1888

Ninety percent of the politicians give the other ten percent a bad reputation.

Henry A. Kissinger, contemporary German-born
U.S. secretary of state

WHENEVER a Republican leaves one side of the aisle and goes to the other, it raises the intelligence quotient of both parties.

Clare Booth Luce, U.S. playwright and ambassador, 1903–1987

I am not a member of any organized party— I'm a Democrat.

Will Rogers, U.S. writer, actor, and humorist, 1879–1935

I HAVE BEEN THINKING THAT I

would make a proposition to my Republican friends: that if they will stop telling lies about the Democrats, we will stop telling the truth about them.

Adlai E. Stevenson, Illinois governor, candidate and UN ambassador, 1900–1965

I'm a right-wing Republican; I'm conservative veering toward reactionary. The big moment of my year comes in October when daylight savings ends, and you can actually turn back the clock.

William Safire, contemporary U.S. journalist

A RADICAL IS A MAN WITH both feet firmly planted—in the air; a conservative is a man with two perfectly good legs who, however, has never learned to walk; a reactionary is a somnambulist walking backwards; a liberal is a man who uses his legs and his hands at the behest of his head.

Franklin D. Roosevelt, U.S. president, 1882–1945

*L*IBERALS feel unworthy of their possessions; conservatives feel they deserve everything they've stolen.

Mort Sahl, contemporary U.S. comedian

Conservative, *n.* A statesman who is enamored of existing evils, as distinguished from the liberal, who wishes to replace them with others.

Ambrose Bierce, U.S. journalist and writer, 1842–1914

THE INHERENT VICE of capitalism is the unequal sharing of blessings. The inherent virtue of socialism is the equal sharing of miseries.

Winston Churchill, British prime minister, 1874–1965

Capitalism works better than it sounds, while socialism sounds better than it works.

Richard M. Nixon, U.S. president, 1913–1994

SOCIALISM IS AN EXPRESSION OF THE DISEASE FOR WHICH IT PURPORTS TO BE THE CURE.

George F. Will, contemporary U.S. journalist

THE FIRST RULE OF DEMOCRACY

is to distrust all leaders who begin to believe their own publicity.

Arthur M. Schlesinger Jr., contemporary U.S. historian

Democracy, as conceived by politicians, is a form of government, that is to say, it is a method of making people do what their leaders wish under the impression that they are doing what they themselves wish.

Bertrand Russell, English mathematician and philosopher, 1872–1970

Democracy is the worst form of government except all those other forms that have been tried from time to time.

Winston Churchill, British prime minister, 1874–1965

Thank heavens we don't get all the government we pay for.
Will Rogers, U.S. writer, actor, and humorist, 1879–1935

The government must be the trustee for the little man because no one else will be. The powerful can usually help themselves—and frequently do.
Adlai E. Stevenson, Illinois governor, presidential candidate and UN ambassador, 1900–1965

GOVERNMENT'S VIEW OF THE ECONOMY COULD BE SUMMED UP IN A FEW SHORT PHRASES: if it moves, tax it; if it keeps moving, regulate it; and if it stops moving, subsidize it.
Ronald Reagan, contemporary U.S. president

THE OPTIMIST PROCLAIMS we live in the best of all possible worlds; and the pessimist fears this is true.

James Branch Cabell, U.S. writer, 1878–1959

Perpetual optimism is annoying. *It is a sign that you are not paying attention.*

Maureen Dowd, contemporary U.S. journalist

Stick with the optimists. It's going to be tough enough even if they're right.

James Reston, U.S. journalist, 1909–1995

41

The so-called nonconformists travel in groups, and woe unto him who doesn't conform.

Eric Hoffer, U.S. longshoreman and writer, 1902–1983

THE REWARD FOR CONFORMITY IS THAT EVERY-ONE LIKES YOU EXCEPT YOURSELF.

Rita Mae Brown, contemporary U.S. writer and poet

It is better to be hated for what you are than loved for what you are not.

André Gide, French writer, 1869–1951

THE coldest winter I ever spent was a summer in San Francisco.

Mark Twain, U.S. writer and humorist, 1835–1910 (attributed)

Nothing so needs reforming as other people's habits.

Mark Twain, U.S. writer and humorist, 1835–1910

TO CEASE SMOKING is the easiest thing. I ought to know. I've done it a thousand times.

Mark Twain, U.S. writer and humorist, 1835–1910

Doctors pour drugs of which they know little, to cure diseases of which they know less, into human beings of whom they know nothing.

Voltaire, French philosopher, 1604–1778

Never go to a doctor whose office plants have died.

Erma Bombeck, U.S. writer and humorist, 1927–1996

*I*F people didn't pick on me, I wouldn't be paranoid.

Anonymous

Just because you're paranoid doesn't mean they're not out to get you.

Anonymous

*I*f you can keep your head when all about you are losing theirs, it's just possible you haven't grasped the situation.

Jean Kerr, U.S. playwright, 1923–2003

We read the world wrong
and say that it deceives us.

Rabindranath Tagore, Indian poet, 1861-1941

MANKIND ARE VERY ODD CREA-TURES: one half censure what they practice, the other half practice what they censure; the rest always say and do as they ought.

Benjamin Franklin, U.S. printer, inventor, and statesman,
1706–1790

An Englishman who was wrecked on a strange shore and wandering along the coast came to a gallows with a victim hanging on it, and fell down on his knees and thanked God that he at last beheld a sign of civilization.

James A. Garfield, U.S. president, 1831–1881

HUMANITY IS DIVIDED INTO TWO CLASSES: the self-seeking, hypocritical minority, and the brainless mob whose destiny is always to be led or driven, as one gets a pig back to the sty by kicking it on the bottom or by rattling a stick inside a swill bucket, according to the needs of the moment.

George Orwell, English writer, 1903–1950

I always divide people into two groups. Those who live by what they know to be a lie, and those who live by what they believe, falsely, to be the truth.

Christopher Hampton, contemporary English playwright

In peace, sons bury their fathers. In war, fathers bury their sons.

Herodotus, Greek historian, fifth century B.C.

You can no more win a war than you can win an earthquake.

Jeannette Rankin, Montana congresswoman, 1880–1973

Someday they'll give a war and nobody will come.

Carl Sandburg, U.S. poet and writer, 1874–1965

Were Moses to go up Mt. Sinai today, the two tablets he'd bring down with him would be aspirin and Prozac.

Joseph A. Califano Jr., contemporary lawyer and secretary of Health, Welfare and Education

Some luck lies in not getting what you thought you wanted but getting what you have, which once you have it you may be smart enough to see is what you would have wanted had you known.

Garrison Keillor, contemporary U.S. writer and humorist

VICTIM: SOMEONE WHO TRUSTS TOO MUCH IN LUCK OR HUMAN KINDNESS.

Jerry Tucker, contemporary U.S. political scientist

Some people reach the top of the ladder only to discover it is leaning against the wrong wall.

Anonymous

The successful people are the ones who can think up things for the rest of the world to keep busy at.

Don Marquis, U.S. journalist and humorist, 1878–1937

THE FASTEST WAY to succeed is to look as if you're playing by other people's rules, while quietly playing by your own.

Michael Korda, contemporary English-born U.S. editor and writer

SUCCESS IN LIFE DEPENDS ON TWO THINGS: luck and pluck, luck in finding someone to pluck.

Ed Wynn, U.S. comedian, 1885–1965

I am a great believer in luck, and I find the harder I work the more I have of it.

Stephen Leacock, Canadian economist and humorist, 1869–1944

Success is just a matter of luck. **ASK ANY FAILURE!**

Earl Wilson, U.S. journalist, 1907–1987

THERE ARE TWO KINDS OF FAILURES: those who thought and never did, and those who did and never thought.

Laurence J. Peter, Canadian academic and writer, 1919–1990

THERE ARE TWO KINDS OF LOSERS: the good loser and those who can't act.

Laurence J. Peter, Canadian academic and writer, 1919–1990

THE young have aspirations that never come to pass, the old have reminiscences of what never happened.

Saki (H. H. Munro), Burmese-born English writer, 1870–1916

The first half of life consists of the capacity to enjoy without the chance; the last half consists of the chance without the capacity.

Mark Twain, U.S. writer and humorist, 1835–1910

THERE WAS NO respect for youth when I was young, and now that I am old there is no respect for age—I missed it coming and going.

J. B. Priestly, English writer and humorist, 1894–1984

Old people are fond of giving good advice; it consoles them for no longer being capable of setting a bad example.

François de La Rochefoucauld, French writer, 1613–1680

It's a sign of age if you feel like the morning after the night before and you haven't been anywhere.

Anonymous

57

*L*ife's tragedy is that we get old too soon and wise too late.

Benjamin Franklin, U.S. printer, inventor, and statesman,
1706–1790

If I'd known I was gonna live this long,
I'd have taken better care of myself.

Eubie Blake, U.S. jazz musician, 1883–1983
(on his one hundredth birthday)

You can live to be a hundred if you give up all the things that make you want to live to a hundred.

Woody Allen, contemporary U.S. writer, humorist, and director

Whom the gods love die young no matter how long they live.

Elbert Hubbard, U.S. writer, editor, and humorist, 1856–1915

To me, old age is always fifteen years older than I am.

Bernard M. Baruch, U.S. financier, 1870–1965 (at age eighty-five)

The less one has to do, the less time one finds to do it in.

Lord Chesterfield, English statesman, 1694–1773

The universe is like a safe to which there is a combination. Unfortunately, the combination is locked up inside the safe.

Peter De Vries, U.S. writer, 1910–1993

We learn from history that we do not learn from history.

Georg Hegel, German philosopher, 1770–1831

HISTORY TEACHES US THAT MEN AND NATIONS BEHAVE WISELY ONCE THEY HAVE EXHAUSTED ALL OTHER ALTERNATIVES.

Abba Eban, South African–born Israeli diplomat, 1915–2002

There are years when nothing happens and years in which centuries happen.

Carlos Fuentes, contemporary Mexican writer

POLITICAL LANGUAGE IS designed to make lies sound truthful and murder respectable, and to give the appearance of solidity to pure wind.

George Orwell, English writer, 1903–1950

I have a sufficient witness to the truth of what I say—my poverty.

Socrates, Greek philosopher, fifth century B.C.

Truth is always subversive.

Anne Lamott, contemporary U.S. writer

The truth is the one thing nobody will believe.

George Bernard Shaw, British playwright and critic, 1856–1950

The most awful thing that one can do is to tell the truth. It's all right in my case because I am not taken seriously.

George Bernard Shaw, British playwright and critic,
1856–1950

THERE ARE ONLY TWO WAYS OF TELLING THE COMPLETE TRUTH—ANONYMOUSLY AND POSTHUMOUSLY.

Thomas Sowell, contemporary U.S. economist

EDITOR: a person employed on a newspaper, whose business it is to separate the wheat from the chaff, *and to see that the chaff is printed.*

Elbert Hubbard, U.S. writer, editor, and humorist, 1856–1915

$\mathcal{G}$OOD people are only half as good, and bad people only half as bad, as other people regard them.

Elbert Hubbard, U.S. writer, editor, and humorist, 1856–1915

To make mistakes is human, but to profit by them is *divine*.

Elbert Hubbard, U.S. writer, editor, and humorist, 1856–1915

THE FELLOW THAT agrees with everything you say is either a fool or he is getting ready to skin you.

Kin Hubbard, U.S. journalist and humorist, 1868–1930

The only way to entertain some folks is to listen to them.

Kin Hubbard, U.S. journalist and humorist, 1868–1930

You can pick out the actors by the glazed look that comes into their eyes when the conversation wanders away from themselves.

Michael Wilding, English actor, 1912–1979 (attributed)

*Y*OU'VE no idea what a poor opinion I have of myself—and how little I deserve it.

W. S. Gilbert, English librettist, 1836–1911

If I only had a little humility, I'd be perfect.

Ted Turner, contemporary U.S. media industry leader

THERE'S ONE THING we ought to let folks find out for themselves, and that's how great we are.

Kin Hubbard, U.S. journalist and humorist, 1868–1930

Virtue would not go nearly so far if vanity did not keep her company.

François de La Rochefoucauld, French writer, 1613–1680

Vanity inclines us to find faults anywhere rather than *in ourselves*.

Samuel Johnson, English writer and lexicographer, 1709–1784

WE often forgive those who bore us, but we cannot forgive those who find us boring.

François de La Rochefoucauld, French writer, 1613–1680

The nice thing about being a celebrity is that when you bore people, they think it's *their fault*.

Henry A. Kissinger, contemporary German-born U.S. secretary of state

To be famous is often to be widely known for what you are not.

Herman Melville, U.S. writer, 1819–1891

M

artyrdom is the only way to become famous without ability.

George Bernard Shaw, British playwright and critic,
1856–1950

THERE IS ONLY one thing in the world worse than being talked about, and that is not being talked about.

Oscar Wilde, English playwright, 1854–1900

THERE ARE ONLY TWO KINDS OF MEN: the righteous who believe themselves sinners and sinners who believe themselves righteous.

Blaise Pascal, French theologian, 1623–1662

The only difference between the saint and the sinner is that every saint has a past, and every sinner has a future.

Oscar Wilde, English playwright, 1854–1900

74

WHEN we resist our passions, it is more on account of their weakness than our strength.

François de La Rochefoucauld, French writer, 1613–1680

The things you want in life come after you no longer want them.

Steve Martin, contemporary U.S. comedian and actor

Good looks build character, as there is so much more temptation to overcome.

Adair Lara, contemporary U.S. journalist

Virtue is insufficient temptation.

George Bernard Shaw, British playwright and critic, 1856–1950

I generally avoid temptation unless I can't resist it.

Mae West, U.S. actor, 1893–1980

76

MARRIAGE has many pains, but celibacy has no pleasures.

Samuel Johnson, English writer and lexicographer, 1709–1784

Marriage is popular because it combines the maximum of temptation with the maximum of opportunity.

George Bernard Shaw, British playwright and critic, 1856–1950

MARRIAGE PROBABLY ORIGINATED
as a straightforward food-for-sex deal among foraging primates. Compatibility was not a big issue, nor, or course, was there any tension over who would control the remote.

Barbara Ehrenreich, contemporary U.S. writer

SOMEONE ONCE ASKED ME WHY

women don't gamble as much as men do, and I gave the common-sensical reply that we don't have as much money. That was a true but incomplete answer. In fact, women's total instinct for gambling is satisfied by marriage.

Gloria Steinem, contemporary U.S. women's rights leader and writer

MARRIAGE IS THE ONLY thing that affords a woman the pleasure of company and the perfect sensation of solitude at the same time.

Helen Rowland, U.S. journalist and humorist, 1875–1950

When I meet a man, I ask myself, **"IF THIS THE MAN I WANT MY CHILDREN TO SPEND WEEKENDS WITH?"**

Rita Rudner, contemporary U.S. comedian

*B*EING divorced is like being hit by a Mack track. If you live through it, you start looking very carefully to the right and to the left.

Jean Kerr, U.S. playwright, 1923–2003

Half of all marriages end in divorce— and then there are the really unhappy ones.

Joan Rivers, contemporary U.S. comedian

THE highest achievement in business is the nearest approach in getting something for nothing.

Thorstein Veblen, U.S. economist, 1857–1929

Corporation, n. An ingenious device for obtaining individual profit without individual responsibility.

Ambrose Bierce, U.S. journalist and writer, 1842–1914

WHICH IS IT? IS MAN ONE OF GOD'S BLUNDERS OR IS GOD ONE OF MAN'S?

Friedrich Nietzsche, German philosopher, 1844–1900

What can you say about a society that says God is dead and Elvis is alive?

Irv Kupcinet, contemporary U.S. journalist

If it turns out that there is a God, I don't think he's evil. But the worst thing that you can say about him is that basically he's an underachiever.

Woody Allen, contemporary U.S. writer, humorist, and director

*G*od's only excuse is that he doesn't exist.

Stendhal (Marie-Henri Beyle), French writer, 1783–1842

If God did not exist, it would be necessary to invent him.

Voltaire, French philosopher, 1604–1778

THE IDEA OF GOD IS slightly more plausible than the alternative proposition that, given enough time, some green slime could write Shakespeare's sonnets.

Tom Stoppard, contemporary Czech-born English playwright

Thanks to God, I'm still an atheist.

Luis Buñuel, French film director, 1900–1983

WE SELDOM REGRET TALKING too little, but very often talking too much. This is a well-known maxim which everybody knows and nobody practices.

Jean de La Bruyère, French moralist, 1645–1696

THOSE WHO KNOW DO NOT TALK,
AND TALKERS DO NOT KNOW.

Lao-tzu, Chinese philosopher, sixth century B.C.

87

He can compress the most words into the smallest ideas of any man I ever met.

Abraham Lincoln, U.S. president, 1809–1865

Half the world is composed of people who have something to say and can't, and the other half who have nothing to say and keep on saying it.

Robert Frost, U.S. poet, 1875–1963

BLESSED IS THE MAN WHO, having

nothing to say, abstains from giving us wordy evidence of the fact.

George Eliot (Mary Ann Evans Cross), English writer, 1819–1880

We all have strength enough to endure the troubles of others.

François de La Rochefoucauld, French writer, 1613–1680

There is always a comforting thought in time of trouble when it is not our trouble.

Don Marquis, U.S. journalist and humorist, 1878–1937

To the envious nothing is more delightful than another's misfortune, and nothing more painful than another's success.

Baruch Spinoza, Dutch philosopher, 1632–1677

It is not enough to succeed. Others must fail.

Gore Vidal, contemporary U.S. writer

THE FICKLENESS OF THE WOMEN

whom I love is only equaled by the infernal constancy of the women who love me.

George Bernard Shaw, British playwright and critic, 1856–1950

The reasonable man adapts himself to the world: the unreasonable one persists in trying to adapt the world to himself. Therefore all progress depends on the unreasonable man.

George Bernard Shaw, British playwright and critic, 1856–1950

THERE ARE TWO TRAGEDIES IN LIFE.

One is to lose your heart's desire. The other is to gain it.

George Bernard Shaw, British playwright and critic, 1856–1950

The nurse—about as big as the small end of nothing whittled down to a fine point, as McMurphy put it later—undid our cuffs and gave McMurphy a cigarette and gave me a stick of gum.

Ken Kesey, U.S. writer, 1935–2001
(in the novel One Flew over the Cuckoo's Nest, *1962)*

IF you talk to God, you are praying; if God talks to you, you have schizophrenia.

Thomas S. Szasz, contemporary Hungarian-born U.S. psychiatrist

Way too much coffee. But if it weren't for the coffee, I'd have no identifiable personality whatsoever.

David Letterman, contemporary U.S. television talk-show host

WHEN I WAS A BOY OF FOURTEEN,

my father was so ignorant I could hardly stand to have the old man around. But when I got to be twenty-one, I was astonished at how much the old man had learned in seven years.

Mark Twain, U.S. writer and humorist, 1835–1910 (attributed)

Chutzpah enables a man who has murdered his mother and father to throw himself on the mercy of the court as an orphan.

Oscar Levant, U.S. pianist, actor, and humorist, 1906–1972 (attributed)

GOING THROUGH A LIFE with a conscience is like driving your car with the brakes on.
Budd Schulberg, contemporary U.S. writer and screenwriter

HERE'S A GOOD RULE OF THUMB: Too clever is dumb.
Ogden Nash, U.S. poet and humorist, 1902–1971

CONSCIENCE: the inner voice which warns us someone may be looking.
H. L. Mencken, U.S. journalist and critic, 1880–1956

There is only one way to achieve
happiness on this terrestrial ball,
And that is to have either a
clear conscience, or none at all.

Ogden Nash, U.S. versifier and
humorist, 1902–1971

When I'm good, I'm very good; but when I'm bad, I'm better.

Mae West, U.S. actor, 1893–1980

They say that "familiarity breeds contempt." I would like to remind you that without a degree of familiarity we could not breed anything.

Winston Churchill, British prime minister, 1874–1965

WHEN I ENTERED MY hotel room last night, I found a strange blonde in my bed. I would stand for none of her nonsense! I gave her exactly twenty-four hours to get out.

Groucho Marx, U.S. comedian, actor, and television personality, 1895–1977

These impossible women! How they get around us! The poet was right: WE CAN'T LIVE WITH THEM, OR WITHOUT THEM!

Aristophanes, Greek playwright, fifth century B.C.

If all the girls at Smith and Bennington were laid end to end, I wouldn't be surprised.

Dorothy Parker, U.S. writer and humorist, 1893–1967

It is better to copulate than never.

Robert A. Heinlein, U.S. writer, 1907–1988

Contraceptives should be used on every conceivable occasion.

Spike Milligan, Irish entertainer and writer, 1918–2002

Many are saved from sin by being so inept at it.

Mignon McLaughlin, contemporary U.S. writer

The worst sin of all is to do well that which shouldn't be done at all.

Alexander Woollcott, U.S. writer, critic, and humorist,
1887–1943

THE secret of respectability is to ignore what you don't understand.

Christopher Morley, U.S. writer and poet, 1890–1957

Respectability, *n.* The social status of people whose sins haven't quite caught up with them.

Edmund H. Volkart, contemporary U.S. writer

Have more than thou showest,
Speak less than thou knowest,
Lend less than thou owest.

*William Shakespeare, English playwright,
1564–1616 (in the play* King Lear, 1605)

They have a plentiful lack of wit.
William Shakespeare, English playwright, 1564–1616
(in the play Hamlet, *1600)*

SHAKESPEARE WROTE GOOD plays, but he wouldn't have succeeded as a Washington correspondent of a New York daily paper. He lacked the requisite fancy and imagination.
Artemus Ward, U.S. writer, lecturer, and humorist, 1834–1867

HOW OFTEN WE RECALL, with regret, that Napoleon once shot at a magazine editor and missed him and killed a publisher. But we remember, with charity, that his intentions were good.

Mark Twain, U.S. writer and humorist, 1835–1910

When I am dead,
I hope it may be said:
His sins were scarlet,
but his books were read.

*Hilaire Belloc, French-born
English writer and poet, 1870–1953*

YOUR manuscript is both good and original; but the part that is good is not original, and the part that is original is not good.

Samuel Johnson, English writer and lexicographer, 1709–1784

In the main, there are two sorts of books: those that no one reads and those that no one ought to read.

H. L. Mencken, U.S. journalist and critic, 1880–1956

The truths of religion are never so well understood as by those who have lost their power of reasoning.

I cherish the greatest respect towards everybody's religious obligations, never mind how comical.

Herman Melville, U.S. writer, 1819–1891

THREE-FOURTHS OF PHILOSOPHY

and literature is the talk of people trying to convince themselves that they really like the cage they were tricked into entering.

Gary Snyder, contemporary U.S. poet

ALL RELIGIONS ARE FOUNDED ON THE FEAR OF THE MANY AND THE CLEVERNESS OF THE FEW.

Stendhal (Marie-Henri Beyle), French writer, 1783–1842

SAY WHAT YOU WILL about the Ten Commandments, you must always come back to the pleasant fact that there are only ten of them.

H. L. Mencken, U.S. journalist and critic, 1880–1956

When the missionaries first came to Africa, they had the Bible and we had the land. They said **"LET US PRAY."** We closed our eyes. When we opened them, we had the Bible and they had the land.

Desmond Tutu, contemporary South African bishop

*A*LL religions die of one disease, that of being found out.

John Morley, English journalist and member of Parliament, 1838–1923

Every day people are straying away from the church and going back to God.

Lenny Bruce, U.S. comedian, 1925–1966

There comes a time in every man's life, and I've had many of them.
Casey Stengel, U.S. baseball player and manager, 1890–1975

If Casey Stengel were alive today, he'd be turning over in his grave.
Yogi Berra, contemporary U.S. baseball player and manager

Ninety percent of baseball is half mental.
Yogi Berra, contemporary U.S. baseball player and manager

NOBODY goes to that restaurant any more —it's too crowded.

Yogi Berra, contemporary U.S. baseball player and manager

When you come to a fork in the road, take it.

Yogi Berra, contemporary U.S. baseball player and manager

I AM AN IDEALIST. I don't know where I'm going, but I'm on my way.

Carl Sandburg, U.S. poet and writer, 1874–1965

IF YOU DON'T KNOW WHERE YOU ARE GOING, YOU WILL PROBABLY END UP SOMEWHERE ELSE.

Laurence J. Peter, Canadian academic and writer, 1919–1990

Too many pieces of music finish too long after the end.

Igor Stravinsky, Russian-born U.S. composer, 1882–1971

I am as old as my tongue and a little older than my teeth.

Jonathan Swift, English clergyman and writer, 1667–1745

THE OPPOSITE OF talking isn't listening. The opposite of talking is waiting.

Fran Lebowitz, contemporary U.S. writer and humorist

There is no such thing as inner peace. There is only nervousness or death.

Fran Lebowitz, contemporary U.S. writer and humorist

Success didn't spoil me; *I've always been insufferable.*

Fran Lebowitz, contemporary U.S. writer and humorist

THERE are two pips in a beaut, four beauts in a lulu, eight lulus in a doozy, and sixteen doozies in a humdinger. No one knows how many humdingers there are in a lollapalooza.

George Carlin, contemporary U.S. comedian

That's as well said as if I had said it myself.
Jonathan Swift, English clergyman and writer, 1667–1745

He was a self-made man who owed his lack of success to nobody.
Joseph Heller, U.S. writer, 1923–1999

There was only one catch and that was Catch-22, which specified that a concern for one's own safety in the face of dangers that were real and immediate was the process of a rational mind. If Orr agreed to fly more combat missions, he was crazy and didn't have to; but if he didn't want to he was sane and had to.
Joseph Heller, U.S. writer, 1923–1999

He had decided to live forever or die in the attempt.
Joseph Heller, U.S. writer, 1923–1999

122

HIS ONE REGRET IN LIFE IS THAT HE IS NOT SOMEONE ELSE.

Woody Allen, contemporary U.S. writer, humorist, and director

Most of the time I don't have much fun; the rest of the time I don't have any fun at all.

Woody Allen, contemporary U.S. writer, humorist, and director

I don't want to achieve immortality through my work. I want to achieve it through not dying.

Woody Allen, contemporary U.S. writer, humorist, and director

ALWAYS remember that you are absolutely unique—just like everyone else.

Margaret Mead, U.S. anthropologist, 1901–1977

We're all in this together—by ourselves.

Lily Tomlin, contemporary U.S. comedian and actor

THE WORST EVIL of all is to leave the ranks of the living before one dies.

Seneca the Younger, Roman philosopher and statesman, first century A.D.

We die only once, and it's for such a long time!

Molière, French playwright, 1622–1672

It's not that I'm afraid to die. I just don't want to be there when it happens.

Woody Allen, contemporary U.S. writer, humorist, and director

UNDERNEATH this flabby exterior is an enormous lack of character.

Oscar Levant, U.S. pianist, actor, and humorist, 1906–1972

I am a deeply superficial person.

Andy Warhol, U.S. artist, 1927–1987

DO INFANTS ENJOY infancy as much as adults enjoy adultery?

George Carlin, contemporary U.S. comedian

If you try to fail and succeed, which have you done?

George Carlin, contemporary U.S. comedian

Most people work just hard enough not to get fired and get paid just enough money not to quit.

George Carlin, contemporary U.S. comedian

It is by the goodness of God that in our country we have those three unspeakably precious things: freedom of speech, freedom of conscience, and the prudence never to practice either of them.

Mark Twain, U.S. writer and humorist, 1835–1910

*N*obody ever went broke underestimating the intelligence of the American public.

H. L. Mencken, U.S. writer, 1880–1956

THE SECRET OF living without frustration and worry is to avoid becoming personally involved in your own life.

Tom Wilson, contemporary U.S. cartoonist

Broadway is a street where people spend money they haven't earned to buy things they don't need to impress people they don't like.

Walter Winchell, U.S. journalist, 1897–1972

IT'S A RECESSION when your neighbor loses his job; it's a depression when you lose your own.

Harry S. Truman, U.S. president, 1884–1972

One of the surprising privileges of intellectuals is that they are free to be scandalously asinine without harming their reputation.

Eric Hoffer, U.S. longshoreman and writer, 1902–1983

THE PURITAN HATED BEAR-BAITING, NOT BECAUSE IT GAVE PAIN TO THE BEAR, BUT BECAUSE IT GAVE PLEASURE TO THE SPECTATORS.

Thomas Babington Macaulay, English historian, 1800–1859

Jealousy is all the fun you think they had.

Erica Jong, contemporary U.S. writer

*P*EOPLE will sometimes forgive you the good
you have done them, but seldom the harm they have done you.

W. Somerset Maugham, English writer, 1874-1965

Expectations are resentments under con-
struction.

Anne Lamott, contemporary U.S. writer

NOTHING IS MORE responsible for the good old days than a bad memory.

Franklin P. Adams, U.S. writer and humorist, 1881–1960

The past ain't what it used to be—it never was.

Anonymous

My interest is in the future because I am going to spend the rest of my life there.

Charles F. Kettering, U.S. inventor, 1976–1958

*T*HE hardest arithmetic to master is that which enables us to count our blessings.

Eric Hoffer, U.S. longshoreman and writer, 1902–1983

May the best day of your past be the worst day of your future.

Chinese Proverb

In times like these, it is helpful to remember that there have always been times like these.

Paul Harvey, contemporary U.S. broadcaster

I now bid you a welcome adoo.

Artemus Ward, U.S. writer, lecturer, and humorist,
1834–1867

LEONARD ROY FRANK, a native of Brooklyn, graduated from the Wharton School of the University of Pennsylvania in 1954. A resident of San Francisco, he managed his own art gallery in the 1970s and has edited a number of books, including *Random House Webster's Quotationary* and *Freedom*. His e-mail address is lfrank@igc.org